TENOR SAX

101 MOST BEAUTIFUL SONGS

Available for
FLUTE, CLARINET, ALTO SAX, TENOR SAX, TRUMPET,
HORN, TROMBONE, VIOLIN, VIOLA, CELLO

ISBN 978-1-5400-4822-6

Visit Hal Leonard Online at
www.halleonard.com

World headquarters, contact:
Hal Leonard
7777 West Bluemound Road
Milwaukee, WI 53213
Email: info@halleonard.com

In Europe, contact:
Hal Leonard Europe Limited
1 Red Place
London, W1K 6PL
Email: info@halleonardeurope.com

In Australia, contact:
Hal Leonard Australia Pty. Ltd.
4 Lentara Court
Cheltenham, Victoria, 3192 Australia
Email: info@halleonard.com.au

CONTENTS

4 Always

5 Always on My Mind

6 And I Love Her

7 And I Love You So

8 And So It Goes

9 Annie's Song

10 Anywhere Is

12 Bein' Green

13 Blackbird

14 The Book of Love

16 The Boxer

17 Bring Him Home

18 By the Time I Get to Phoenix

19 Candle in the Wind

20 A Child Is Born

22 City of Stars

21 (They Long to Be) Close to You

24 Come Sunday

25 Crazy

26 Crying

28 Daughters

27 Dream a Little Dream of Me

30 Easy Living

31 Eternal Flame

32 Eternally

33 Every Breath You Take

34 (Everything I Do) I Do It For You

35 Feeling Good

36 For All We Know

37 Gabriel's Oboe

38 Good Night

39 Goodnight, Sweetheart, Goodnight
(Goodnight, It's Time to Go)

40 Have I Told You Lately

42 Heal the World

41 Hello

44 Here, There and Everywhere

45 Highland Cathedral

46 I Have a Dream

48 I Left My Heart in San Francisco

49 I Will

50 I'll Be Around

51 I'll Be Seeing You

52 I've Dreamed of You

54 In My Room

56 Just Give Me a Reason

55 La vie en rose (Take Me to Your Heart Again)

58 Lady in Red

59 Let It Be Me (Je t'appartiens)

60 Lost in Your Eyes

62 Love Me Tender

63 Loving You

64 Lullabye (Goodnight, My Angel)

65 Mia & Sebastian's Theme

66 Michelle

67 Mona Lisa

68 My Foolish Heart

69 My Funny Valentine

70 My Valentine

71 My Way

72 Nancy with the Laughing Face

73 Nature Boy

74 Never Enough

76 A Nightingale Sang in Berkeley Square

77 Perfect

78 Photograph

80 The Place Where Lost Things Go

81 Rainy Days and Mondays

82 Release Me

83 Rewrite the Stars

84 Sailing

86 Scarborough Fair/Canticle

88 Shallow

90 She's Always a Woman

89 Since I Don't Have You

92 Smile

93 Smoke Gets in Your Eyes

94 Something Wonderful

95 Somewhere

96 The Sound of Silence

97 Stardust

98 Strangers in the Night

99 Sway (Quien será)

100 Tennessee Waltz

101 (There Is) No Greater Love

102 They Say It's Wonderful

103 Three Times a Lady

104 Time to Say Goodbye

106 True Colors

107 Truly

108 Unexpected Song

110 We've Got Tonight

109 We've Only Just Begun

112 What a Wonderful World

113 Wonderful Tonight

114 Yester-Me, Yester-You, Yesterday

115 Yesterday Once More

116 Yesterday, When I Was Young (Hier encore)

117 You Are the Sunshine of My Life

118 You're the Inspiration

119 Young at Heart

120 Your Song

ALWAYS

TENOR SAX

Words and Music by
IRVING BERLIN

ALWAYS ON MY MIND

TENOR SAX

Words and Music by WAYNE THOMPSON,
MARK JAMES and JOHNNY CHRISTOPHER

AND I LOVE HER

TENOR SAX

Words and Music by JOHN LENNON
and PAUL McCARTNEY

AND I LOVE YOU SO

TENOR SAX

Words and Music by
DON McLEAN

Moderately

AND SO IT GOES

TENOR SAX

Words and Music by
BILLY JOEL

Slow Ballad, with much rubato

ANNIE'S SONG

TENOR SAX

Words and Music by
JOHN DENVER

ANYWHERE IS

TENOR SAX

Words and Music by ENYA,
NICKY RYAN and ROMA RYAN

D.S. al Coda

CODA

BEIN' GREEN

TENOR SAX

Words and Music by
JOE RAPOSO

Slowly, reflectively

BLACKBIRD

TENOR SAX

Words and Music by JOHN LENNON
and PAUL McCARTNEY

Slowly and smoothly

THE BOOK OF LOVE

TENOR SAX

Words and Music by
STEPHIN MERRITT

CODA

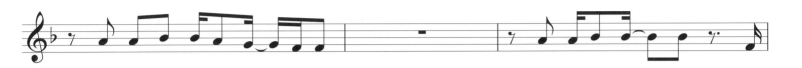

THE BOXER

TENOR SAX

Words and Music by
PAUL SIMON

BRING HIM HOME
from LES MISÉRABLES

TENOR SAX

Music by CLAUDE-MICHEL SCHÖNBERG
Lyrics by HERBERT KRETZMER and ALAIN BOUBLIL

Moderately slow

BY THE TIME I GET TO PHOENIX

TENOR SAX

Words and Music by
JIMMY WEBB

CANDLE IN THE WIND

TENOR SAX

Words and Music by ELTON JOHN
and BERNIE TAUPIN

A CHILD IS BORN

TENOR SAX

By THAD JONES

(They Long to Be)
CLOSE TO YOU

TENOR SAX

Lyrics by HAL DAVID
Music by BURT BACHARACH

CITY OF STARS
from LA LA LAND

TENOR SAX

Music by JUSTIN HURWITZ
Lyrics by BENJ PASEK & JUSTIN PAUL

Slower

rit.

COME SUNDAY
from BLACK, BROWN & BEIGE

TENOR SAX

By DUKE ELLINGTON

CRAZY

TENOR SAX

Words and Music by
WILLIE NELSON

CRYING

TENOR SAX

Words and Music by ROY ORBISON
and JOE MELSON

Moderately slow, with feeling

DREAM A LITTLE DREAM OF ME

TENOR SAX

Words by GUS KAHN
Music by WILBUR SCHWANDT
and FABIAN ANDREE

DAUGHTERS

TENOR SAX

Words and Music by
JOHN MAYER

EASY LIVING
Theme from the Paramount Picture EASY LIVING

TENOR SAX

Words and Music by LEO ROBIN
and RALPH RAINGER

ETERNAL FLAME

TENOR SAX

Words and Music by BILLY STEINBERG,
TOM KELLY and SUSANNA HOFFS

ETERNALLY

TENOR SAX

Words by GEOFFREY PARSONS
Music by CHARLES CHAPLIN

EVERY BREATH YOU TAKE

TENOR SAX

Music and Lyrics by
STING

(EVERYTHING I DO) I DO IT FOR YOU

from the Motion Picture ROBIN HOOD: PRINCE OF THIEVES

TENOR SAX

Written by MICHAEL KAMEN

FEELING GOOD

from THE ROAR OF THE GREASEPAINT – THE SMELL OF THE CROWD

TENOR SAX

Words and Music by LESLIE BRICUSSE
and ANTHONY NEWLEY

FOR ALL WE KNOW

TENOR SAX

Words by SAM M. LEWIS
Music by J. FRED COOTS

GABRIEL'S OBOE
from the Motion Picture THE MISSION

TENOR SAX

Words and Music by
ENNIO MORRICONE

GOOD NIGHT

TENOR SAX

Words and Music by JOHN LENNON
and PAUL McCARTNEY

Slowly and dreamily

GOODNIGHT, SWEETHEART, GOODNIGHT
(Goodnight, It's Time to Go)

TENOR SAX

Words and Music by JAMES HUDSON
and CALVIN CARTER

Moderately

HAVE I TOLD YOU LATELY

TENOR SAX

Words and Music by
VAN MORRISON

HELLO

TENOR SAX

Words and Music by
LIONEL RICHIE

HEAL THE WORLD

TENOR SAX

Words and Music by
MICHAEL JACKSON

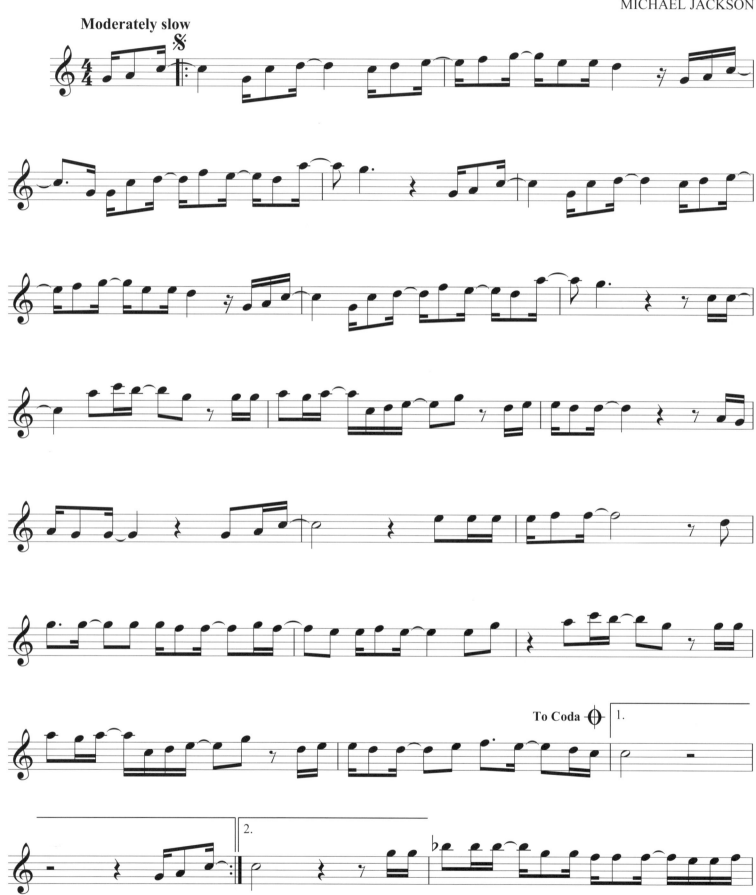

D.S. al Coda

CODA

(small notes optional)

HERE, THERE AND EVERYWHERE

TENOR SAX

Words and Music by JOHN LENNON
and PAUL McCARTNEY

HIGHLAND CATHEDRAL

TENOR SAX

By MICHAEL KORB
and ULRICH ROEVER

Stately March, in 2

I HAVE A DREAM
from MAMMA MIA!

TENOR SAX

Words and Music by BENNY ANDERSSON
and BJÖRN ULVAEUS

D.S. al Coda

CODA

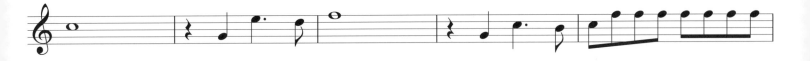

I LEFT MY HEART IN SAN FRANCISCO

TENOR SAX

Words by DOUGLASS CROSS
Music by GEORGE CORY

I WILL

TENOR SAX

Words and Music by JOHN LENNON
and PAUL McCARTNEY

I'LL BE AROUND

TENOR SAX

Words and Music by
ALEC WILDER

Slowly, with expression

I'LL BE SEEING YOU

from RIGHT THIS WAY

TENOR SAX

Written by IRVING KAHAL
and SAMMY FAIN

Moderately slow

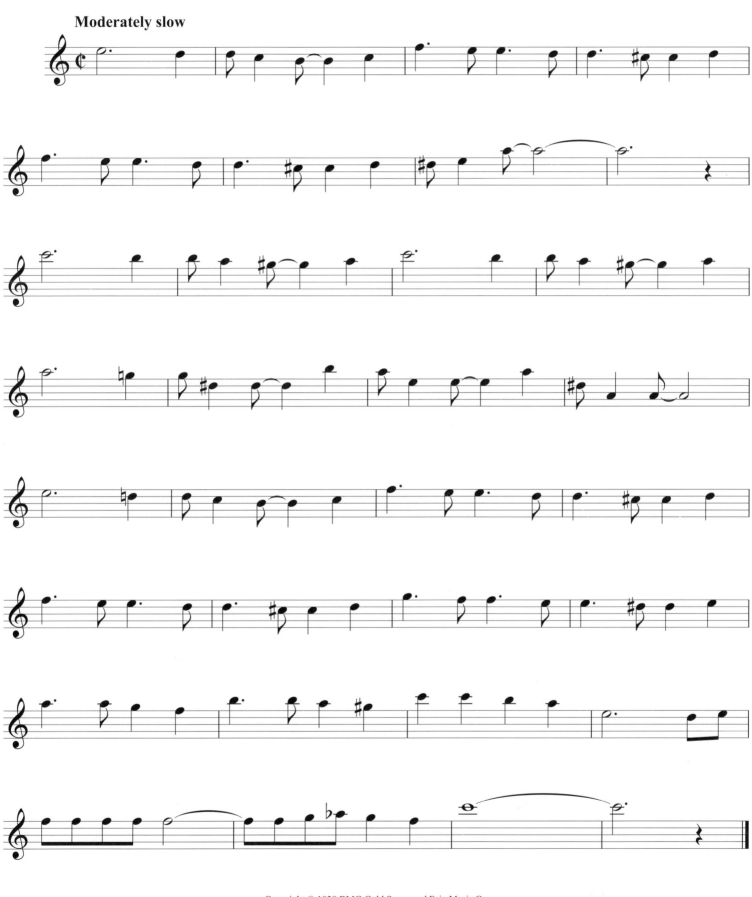

I'VE DREAMED OF YOU

TENOR SAX

Words and Music by ANN HAMPTON CALLAWAY
and ROLF LOVLAND

IN MY ROOM

TENOR SAX

Words and Music by BRIAN WILSON
and GARY USHER

LA VIE EN ROSE
(Take Me to Your Heart Again)

TENOR SAX

Original French Lyrics by EDITH PIAF
Music by LUIGUY
English Lyrics by MACK DAVID

Slowly, with expression

JUST GIVE ME A REASON

TENOR SAX

Words and Music by ALECIA MOORE,
JEFF BHASKER and NATE RUESS

CODA

LADY IN RED

TENOR SAX

Words and Music by
CHRIS DeBURGH

Moderately slow

LET IT BE ME
(Je t'appartiens)

TENOR SAX

English Words by MANN CURTIS
French Words by PIERRE DeLANOE
Music by GILBERT BECAUD

LOST IN YOUR EYES

TENOR SAX

Words and Music by
DEBORAH GIBSON

LOVE ME TENDER

TENOR SAX

Words and Music by ELVIS PRESLEY
and VERA MATSON

LOVING YOU

TENOR SAX

Words and Music by JERRY LEIBER
and MIKE STOLLER

Slowly, with a beat

LULLABYE
(Goodnight, My Angel)

TENOR SAX

Words and Music by
BILLY JOEL

Rubato, gently

MIA & SEBASTIAN'S THEME

from LA LA LAND

TENOR SAX

Music by
JUSTIN HURWITZ

MICHELLE

TENOR SAX

Words and Music by JOHN LENNON
and PAUL McCARTNEY

MONA LISA

from the Paramount Picture CAPTAIN CAREY, U.S.A.

TENOR SAX

Words and Music by JAY LIVINGSTON
and RAY EVANS

MY FOOLISH HEART

TENOR SAX

Words by NED WASHINGTON
Music by VICTOR YOUNG

MY FUNNY VALENTINE

from BABES IN ARMS

TENOR SAX

Words by LORENZ HART
Music by RICHARD RODGERS

MY VALENTINE

TENOR SAX

Words and Music by
PAUL McCARTNEY

MY WAY

TENOR SAX

English Words by PAUL ANKA
Original French Words by GILLES THIBAULT
Music by JACQUES REVAUX and CLAUDE FRANCOIS

NANCY WITH THE LAUGHING FACE

TENOR SAX

Words by PHIL SILVERS
Music by JAMES VAN HEUSEN

NATURE BOY

TENOR SAX

Words and Music by
EDEN AHBEZ

NEVER ENOUGH
from THE GREATEST SHOWMAN

TENOR SAX

Words and Music by BENJ PASEK
and JUSTIN PAUL

A NIGHTINGALE SANG IN BERKELEY SQUARE

TENOR SAX

Lyric by ERIC MASCHWITZ
Music by MANNING SHERWIN

PERFECT

TENOR SAX

Words and Music by
ED SHEERAN

PHOTOGRAPH

TENOR SAX

Words and Music by ED SHEERAN,
JOHNNY McDAID, MARTIN PETER HARRINGTON
and TOM LEONARD

(small note optional)

THE PLACE WHERE LOST THINGS GO
from MARY POPPINS RETURNS

TENOR SAX

Music by MARC SHAIMAN
Lyrics by SCOTT WITTMAN and MARC SHAIMAN

RAINY DAYS AND MONDAYS

TENOR SAX

Lyrics by PAUL WILLIAMS
Music by ROGER NICHOLS

RELEASE ME

TENOR SAX

Words and Music by ROBERT YOUNT,
EDDIE MILLER and DUB WILLIAMS

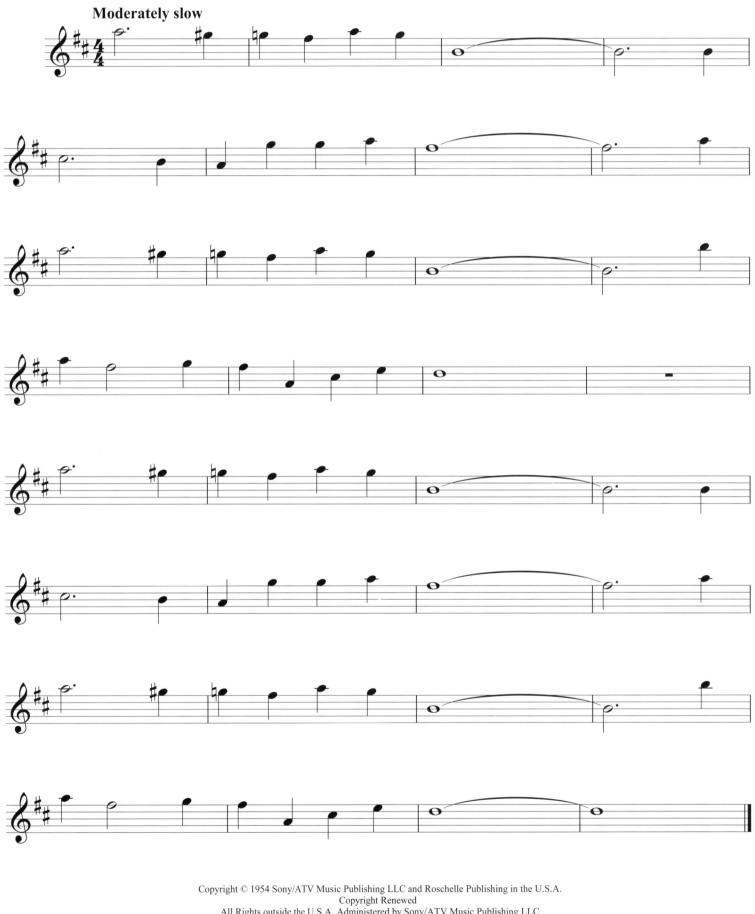

REWRITE THE STARS

from THE GREATEST SHOWMAN

TENOR SAX

Words and Music by BENJ PASEK
and JUSTIN PAUL

SAILING

TENOR SAX

Words and Music by
CHRISTOPHER CROSS

SCARBOROUGH FAIR/CANTICLE

TENOR SAX

Arrangement and Original Counter Melody by
PAUL SIMON and ARTHUR GARFUNKEL

SHALLOW
from A STAR IS BORN

TENOR SAX

Words and Music by STEFANI GERMANOTTA,
MARK RONSON, ANDREW WYATT
and ANTHONY ROSSOMANDO

Moderately

SINCE I DON'T HAVE YOU

TENOR SAX

Words and Music by JAMES BEAUMONT,
JANET VOGEL, JOSEPH VERSCHAREN,
WALTER LESTER, LENNIE MARTIN,
JOSEPH ROCK and JOHN TAYLOR

Slowly, with a strong, rockin' beat

SHE'S ALWAYS A WOMAN

TENOR SAX

Words and Music by
BILLY JOEL

Quickly, in 1

SMILE
Theme from MODERN TIMES

TENOR SAX

Words by JOHN TURNER and GEOFFREY PARSONS
Music by CHARLES CHAPLIN

Moderately, with great warmth

SMOKE GETS IN YOUR EYES

from ROBERTA

TENOR SAX

Words by OTTO HARBACH
Music by JEROME KERN

Moderately

SOMETHING WONDERFUL

from THE KING AND I

TENOR SAX

Lyrics by OSCAR HAMMERSTEIN II
Music by RICHARD RODGERS

SOMEWHERE

from WEST SIDE STORY

TENOR SAX

Lyrics by STEPHEN SONDHEIM
Music by LEONARD BERNSTEIN

THE SOUND OF SILENCE

TENOR SAX

Words and Music by
PAUL SIMON

STARDUST

TENOR SAX

Words by MITCHELL PARISH
Music by HOAGY CARMICHAEL

STRANGERS IN THE NIGHT
adapted from A MAN COULD GET KILLED

TENOR SAX

Words by CHARLES SINGLETON
and EDDIE SNYDER
Music by BERT KAEMPFERT

SWAY
(Quien será)

TENOR SAX

English Words by NORMAN GIMBEL
Spanish Words and Music by PABLO BELTRÁN RUIZ
and LUIS DEMETRIO TRACONIS MOLINA

TENNESSEE WALTZ

TENOR SAX

Words and Music by REDD STEWART
and PEE WEE KING

(THERE IS) NO GREATER LOVE

TENOR SAX

Words by MARTY SYMES
Music by ISHAM JONES

THEY SAY IT'S WONDERFUL

from the Stage Production ANNIE GET YOUR GUN

TENOR SAX

Words and Music by
IRVING BERLIN

THREE TIMES A LADY

TENOR SAX

Words and Music by
LIONEL RICHIE

TIME TO SAY GOODBYE

TENOR SAX

Words by LUCIO QUARANTOTTO
and FRANK PETERSON
Music by FRANCESCO SARTORI

TRUE COLORS

TENOR SAX

Words and Music by BILLY STEINBERG
and TOM KELLY

TRULY

TENOR SAX

Words and Music by
LIONEL RICHIE

UNEXPECTED SONG
from SONG & DANCE

TENOR SAX

Music by ANDREW LLOYD WEBBER
Lyrics by DON BLACK

Gently

(small notes optional)

WE'VE ONLY JUST BEGUN

TENOR SAX

Words and Music by ROGER NICHOLS
and PAUL WILLIAMS

WE'VE GOT TONIGHT

TENOR SAX

Words and Music by
BOB SEGER

WHAT A WONDERFUL WORLD

TENOR SAX

Words and Music by GEORGE DAVID WEISS
and BOB THIELE

WONDERFUL TONIGHT

TENOR SAX

Words and Music by
ERIC CLAPTON

YESTER-ME, YESTER-YOU, YESTERDAY

TENOR SAX

Words by RON MILLER
Music by BRYAN WELLS

YESTERDAY ONCE MORE

TENOR SAX

Words and Music by JOHN BETTIS
and RICHARD CARPENTER

YESTERDAY, WHEN I WAS YOUNG
(Hier Encore)

TENOR SAX

English Lyric by HERBERT KRETZMER
Original French Text and Music by CHARLES AZNAVOUR

Moderate tempo

YOU ARE THE SUNSHINE OF MY LIFE

TENOR SAX

Words and Music by
STEVIE WONDER

YOU'RE THE INSPIRATION

TENOR SAX

Words and Music by PETER CETERA
and DAVID FOSTER

YOUNG AT HEART

from YOUNG AT HEART

TENOR SAX

Words by CAROLYN LEIGH
Music by JOHNNY RICHARDS

YOUR SONG

TENOR SAX

Words and Music by ELTON JOHN
and BERNIE TAUPIN